BABY MAGIC
EXPLORING FAMILIES
AND THE MIRACLE OF BIRTH!

WRITTEN BY HUGRUN KRISTJANSDOTTIR

ILLUSTRATIONS BY HUGRUN KRISTJANSDOTTIR
MIDJORNEY AND DALL-E

Baby Magic
© Hugrun Kristjansdottir

English:
Helga Soffia Einarsdottir

Illustrations:
Hugrun Kristjansdottir
Midjorney
Dall-e

Printed by:
KDP Amazon

All Rights Reserved. Except as permitted under current legislation no part of this work may be photocopied, stored in a retrieval system, published, performed in public, adapted, broadcast, transmitted, recorded, or reproduced in any form or by any means, without the prior permission of the copyright owner.

Luzern, Switzerland, 2023
All rights reserved.

BABY MAGIC
EXPLORING FAMILIES
AND THE MIRACLE OF BIRTH!

BY HUGRUN KRISTJANSDOTTIR

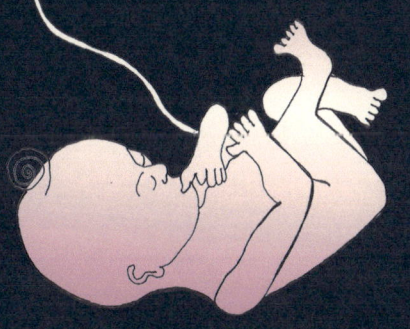

I don't know how I know it, and yet I'm quite sure. Just now something amazing is happening. At exactly this moment a sperm cell is crawling into an egg. This has in fact happened a hundred million times before and will definitely happen a hundred million times again, but this time it's really special. At least for me.

My sperm cell and my egg
are finally merging. If successful,
I will be born into the world
as a baby.

Men have sperm and women have eggs, and each and every child in the world is created from a sperm cell and an egg.

I get half of myself from the sperm cell and the other half from the egg and yet I have many talents that no one knows from where they come. I have no idea how I will look and I don't know how my family will be assembled.

I don't even know whether I'll be a boy or a girl!

Usually a man and a woman create a child by making love. Love is one of the most baffling mysteries of life. It's a force that makes two people long to be together all the time. People in love want to touch and kiss and merge into one.

Two women can have a baby together if a man gives them sperm. Two men can have a baby together if a woman is willing to carry the child.

Some people fall in love when they are young and stay in love forever. Others meet later in life and are perhaps only in love for a few years. Some people fall in love many times, while others only fall in love once in a life time. And then there are those who fall in love for a single night.

You can make a baby
even though love lasts only
a couple of hours.

Most children have one mum and one dad. But some have two mums, while others have two dads. And some children have just a mum and no dad. Or just a dad and no mum. Or two moms and two dads. The possibilities really are endless!

The reason is that even though all children are made from a sperm cell from a man and an egg from a woman, the man or woman in question will not necessarily become the baby's parents.

If two people can't have a baby together, they can ask a doctor to combine the sperm and egg. The egg and sperm cell are put together in a Petri dish and when the egg is fertilized it is placed into a woman's womb.

It usually takes nine months from the time a sperm cell crawls into an egg until the baby is ready to be born. The fertilized egg, or embryo, has to divide into hands and feet, heart and lungs, eyes and ears. There are so many organs to make that it is impossible to name them all!

When a baby comes into the world
it will be absolutely unique.

While I change from an embryo into a little baby, a special bond will form between me and the people that will become the most important people in my life.

They are going to take care of me and love me more than anything in the world. I will love them back and call them mum or dad.

I'm not the only one who will be unique. I'll have a family that will be like no other.

"I dream of visiting Paris," Angela said, dancing in circles. "And I wish I could speak French as beautifully as Brigitte Bardot."

"Even though you don't speak French, you are a million times lovelier than Brigitte Bardot," said Carl. "And you have a better voice than Edith Piaf."

They danced together into the night. The following morning they found out they were going to have a baby.

"Please run to the bakery and get me a caramel doughnut," she begged. He nodded.

On the way back he bought a romper-suit that seemed to fit to a doll. Or a tiny, newborn baby.

I am the size of an uncrushed peppercorn and I have eyes but no eyelids. Yesterday my heart beat for the very first time. Wow, that really startled me! But who are Brigitte Bardot and Edith Piaf?

1 MONTH!

"You won't believe what's happened!" James yelled, running towards Derek. "Sarah just called and she is two months pregnant."

James gasped, trying to catch his breath. He bent his head between his legs and took a deep breath. Then he smiled and whispered: "We're going to be dads."

They held hands and looked into each other's eyes. "Dads," they said both at once.

2 MONTHS!

I was made from a sperm cell from daddy James and an egg from Sarah. I am the size of a grape and I have fingers but I can't spread them apart because they are webbed. My organs are slowly developing and it's quite exhausting. That's why I need to sleep a lot.

"I think green is more beautiful than yellow," said Amy. "It's also scientifically proven that green is easier on the eye."

"What do you mean by easier on the eye?" said Erica curious.

"It's right in the middle of the colour spectrum," Amy explained passionately. "The colour spectrum covers all the colours of the world, just like the alphabet contains all the letters."

"Well, then we'll paint the nursery green." Erica planted a kiss on Amy. "Green may be easy on the eyes but I can't take my eyes off you."

I'm inside the belly of mummy Amy, but my mums got sperm from a stranger. I'm the size of a thumb and I have toes and even eyelids. All my organs are ready and I can wiggle my toes, clench my fist and pout my lips.

3 MONTHS!

Towards the end of summer Julie made two discoveries, one was that she was pregnant and the other was that she would raise her baby on her own.

Julie watched the winter sunset. Her mind was racing and her heart beat faster. "I'm having a baby," she thought to herself and smiled. "My baby is due in spring."

My mum will raise me by herself, but maybe I'll meet my dad someday. I have hair now and I'm constantly moving. I also have earlobes and nails. My joints now function pretty well and I do karate kicks many times a day. I'm as big as a TV remote.

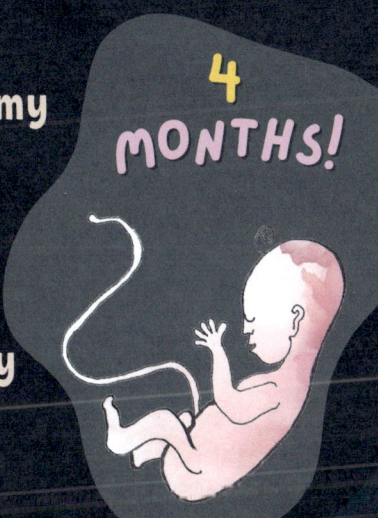

4 MONTHS!

"Shakira, my love" John began carefully. "I was lonely and sad before I met you. You are my best friend and my soul mate. I love you more than words can say. Will you be my wife? "

Shakira smiled. Her black eyes shimmering like stars. "Of course," she said softly and nothing more. They sealed their love with a kiss.

I can now hear sounds through the belly and I detect light and shadows through my eyelids even though I can't open my eyes. I'm always on the move and when I'm bored I suck my thumb. I am as big as a milk carton!

5 MONTHS!

It was New Year's Eve and everything had changed. In one corner of Emily's teen-queen room was a neat, white painted crib and on top of it was a folded quilt. Lying on a pile on the floor was a half knitted baby body-suit and a much used, black mobile phone. The clock struck twelve at midnight. At that very moment the phone stirred. The message from Benny was short and sweet: "I love you, Baby."

My mum and dad are sometimes together and sometimes not. They are 18 years old and live with their parents. Or, uhm, my mum lives with her parents and my dad with his. I'm slightly larger than a rabbit and sometimes I get hiccups!

6 MONTHS!

"Most women rub their belly when they are expecting, but I read the same e-mail over and over," Rose said pensively. "What troubles me the most is how very far away she is. When I read the e-mail she feels closer. Last night I dreamt of her and she was crying so hard that I started to cry myself."

Rose closed her eyes. She could almost smell the scent of her hair, touch her soft skin and hear the sounds of a foreign language out in the street.

"Sleep, baby, sleep
Your father tends the sheep
Your mother shakes the dreamland tree
And from it fall sweet dreams for thee."

I'm inside the belly of my biological mother because my mum and dad are going to adopt me. Now I clearly feel when someone touches me through the belly. I am the same size as a puffin and I am in my birth position. I'm completely upside down!

7 MONTHS!

"Do you think it's possible to be too happy?" Judy asked looking at Stuart.

"Well," Stuart pondered. "When I was little, my grandmother took me to the amusement park. We went a few rounds on the Ferris wheel and then we saw the most magnificent fireworks. That night I lay awake. Granny said it was the sugar-rush, but that wasn't the reason." Stuart smiled. "I couldn't sleep because I was too happy."

Stuart is my mum's boyfriend and my step-dad. My dad is there too. He's always there for me and makes sure he is always available. The womb has become so tight that I can hardly move anymore.

8 MONTHS!

"Do you remember when we thought we could never have a baby and we cried ourselves to sleep?" Robert asked. "We were always at the hospital, all those ovulation tests and sperm tests, all those countless fertility measures and injection treatments, all the drugs and the waiting. And here you are so incredibly pregnant and extremely beautiful. I sometimes have to pinch myself in the arm because I can't believe this is really happening. I cry myself to sleep and cry out of joy and endless happiness and infinite love."

Mary nodded and smiled. "Do I ever remember."

9 MONTHS!

Mum and dad had help creating me. It took a loooooong time but fortunately they succeeded in the end. But now I'm ready to come into the world. I'm just going to take a little nap before the big event.

In nine months I've transformed from a tiny cell into a small infant. The most remarkable thing of all is that even though I look similar to other newborns, and maybe to someone in my family, there will never be another person who will be exactly like me.

We all are born naked, no one stands out, and yet it's absolutely certain that each and every one of us is unique.

I am special and so are you.

My favourite things are warm milk and love. Preferably both at the same time.

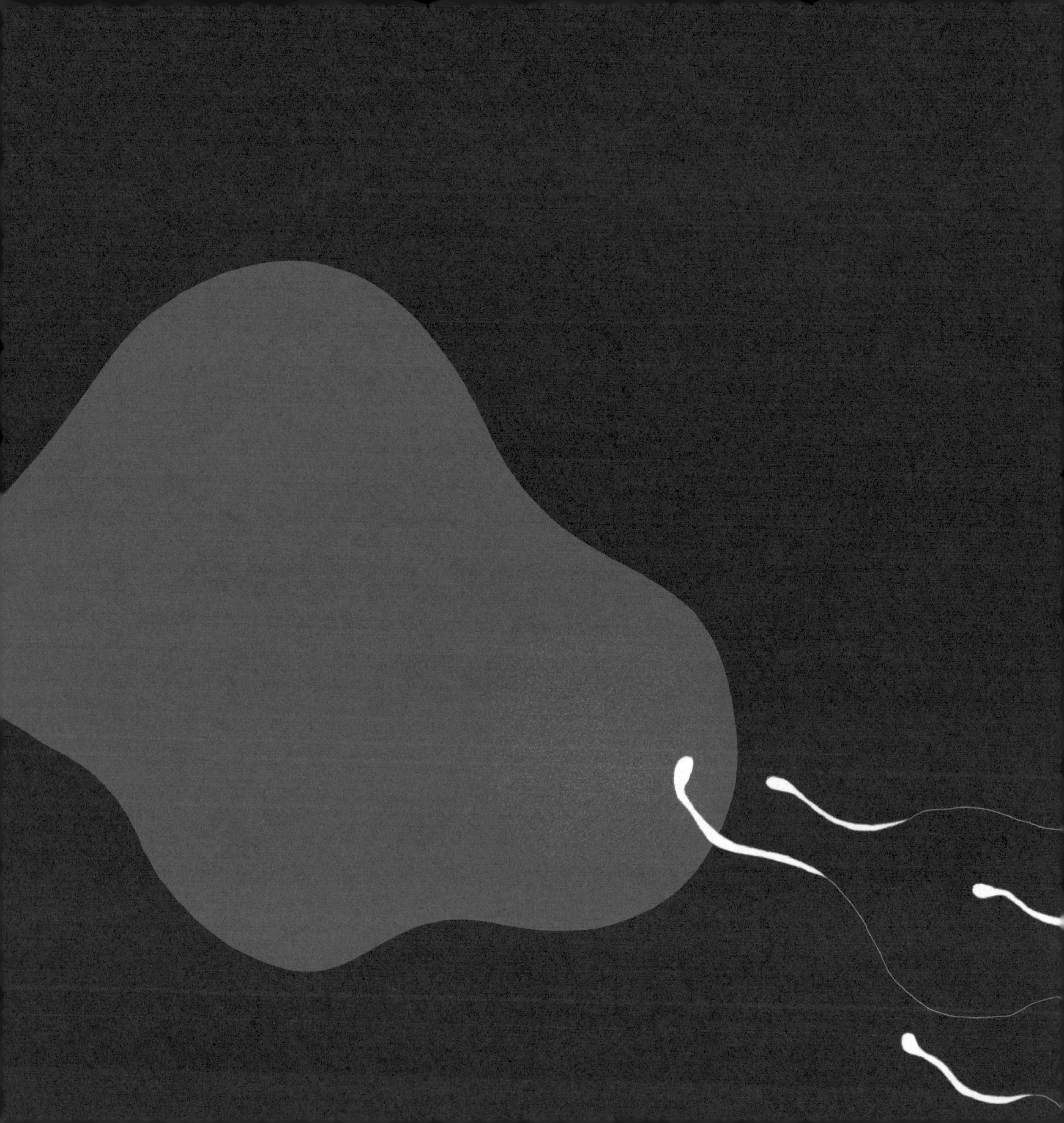

THE END

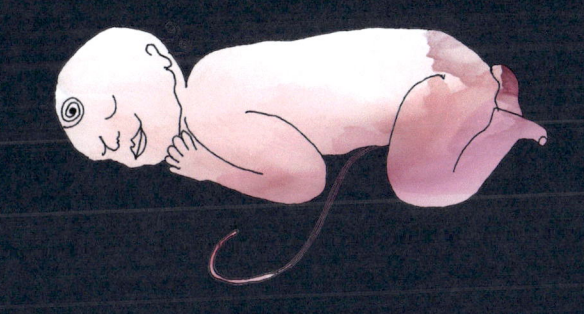

About the Author

Hugrún Hrönn Kristjánsdóttir is from Reykjavik, Iceland. She published her first novel, Stolen Voices, in 2010. Baby Magic is her second book.

Hugrún has a BA degree in Icelandic and an MBA. She holds a Clinical Master's in Addiction Counseling from The University of South Dakota and is a licensed Alcohol and Drug Counselor, endorsed by The Directorate of Health in Iceland. She has extensive experience, both as a healthcare practitioner and a proficient manager in the addiction recovery field,

Made in the USA
Columbia, SC
04 December 2023